20 (

Amazing ...en
and How They Met
Jesus

PUBLISHED BY
KRATOS PUBLISHER

20 ORDINARY AMAZING WOMEN AND HOW THEY MET JESUS

Copyright © 2024

Published by: Kratos Publisher

AMP

Scripture quotations taken from the Amplified® Bible (AMP), Copyright © 2015 by The Lockman Foundation. Used by permission.

NIV

Scriptures taken from the Holy Bible, New International Version®, NIV®. Copyright © 1973, 1978, 1984, 2011 by Biblica, Inc.™ Used by permission of Zondervan. All rights reserved worldwide. www.zondervan.com The "NIV" and "New International Version" are trademarks registered in the United States Patent and Trademark Office by Biblica, Inc.™

TPT

Scripture quotations marked TPT are from The Passion Translation®. Copyright © 2017, 2018, 2020 by Passion & Fire Ministries, Inc. Used by permission. All rights reserved. ThePassionTranslation.com.

ESV

Scripture quotations are from The ESV® Bible (The Holy Bible, English Standard Version®), © 2001 by Crossway, a publishing ministry of Good News Publishers. Used by permission. All rights reserved.

ISBN: 9798878089661

Contents

Introduction

As we delve into these pages, we discover that an extraordinary depth of faith, love, and transformation can lie within a seemingly simple life. Whether by a well, in a crowded marketplace, or the quiet solitude of their homes, these women found themselves touched by a divine presence that transcended the ordinary and infused their lives with purpose and meaning.

Each story is a testament to the universality of the human experience and the enduring relevance of Jesus' teachings. These narratives remind us that the extraordinary can be found in the most commonplace moments and that the divine often reveals itself amid our everyday lives.

Join us on this exploration of faith as we encounter the sacred within the mundane and witness the profound impact of divine grace on the lives of twenty ordinary yet

amazing women. Their stories resonate across time and space, inviting us to reflect on our own journeys and consider the transformative power that awaits in the most unexpected encounters with the divine.

I

Shola Alabi

My upbringing:

I was raised in a Christian family. My parents were members of the Anglican Church, which is not dissimilar to the Church of England. We attended Church every Sunday, where my Christian teaching began. As a child, I was very inquisitive and always asked questions. I would read the Bible in my quest for answers.

When I reached my teenage years, I began participating in events organised by the Evangelical group within our family church. I then understood what being born again really meant. It was not until I left home for university that I eventually gave my life to Christ publicly.

When I met Jesus:

When I arrived at university, I knew I had to declare my faith publicly. Though I had a knowledge of Christ and had personally received Him, there was more to discover.

On this fateful day, I went to Church with a friend I didn't know had been praying for me. As the preacher was delivering the sermon, he made an altar call asking for anyone who would like to receive Jesus. I felt a push (which I now know was the Holy Spirit) and got up before walking down the aisle to the front. From that day onwards, my life has been embodied in Christ.

How it changed my life:

I am now aware of God's presence, which gives me confidence that my life is in His hands. I have the gift of the Holy Spirit. I have a Father who loves me unconditionally. I have seen answers to prayers, which have reaffirmed my faith. I am hopeful and trust in God.

I look forward to speaking to Him and hearing Him speak back to me. I would also love for you to experience this life-changing encounter as I did.

II

Renesia Keymist

<u>My upbringing:</u>

My upbringing was your typical Afro-Caribbean upbringing: tough love, moral standards, expectations, and religion. I was privileged to have two hardworking parents at home who did everything possible to ensure my sibling and I had what we needed. I was born in Guyana, then moved to St. Lucia at six and then to England at eleven, where I now reside permanently. I heard and experienced numerous things about spirituality and was aware of God from a young age.

<u>When I met Jesus:</u>

I learned of Jesus at six when I moved to St. Lucia. My father was given a gospel CD, and from then on, I have loved music. I played the CD repeatedly until I learnt the lyrics for every song so I could sing them in church. I spent numerous days belting out these worship songs.

Eventually, it caught the attention of two of my neighbours, and both invited me to come to their church. I got permission from my mother, and off I went. I visited both the Methodist church and the Seventh Day Adventist church. I loved the worship, bible stories, reading and learning at the time and was captivated by the stories of Jesus' miracles. It was as if He planted something in my heart that told me God was real, and no one could tell me otherwise. From the tender age of six, I knew my heart was His. I heard the story of salvation and prayed to accept the Lord into my heart, leading me to attend more Christian events.

After leaving St. Lucia and moving to England, I tried to look for churches and ended up at one with an amazing youth club. Around that time, I was having very vivid and frequent spiritual encounters through dreams and sleep paralysis. I struggled with a lot of fear and anxiety. I

reached out to the church for help, but they were unsure of what to do with me, so I stopped going and decided that I didn't need a church and that my faith in God was enough. In my teenage years, my spiritual experiences had intensified to a point where I was terrified of the dark and even sleeping at night. I was given a flyer for a concert I believed to be secular but was a church concert. I was disappointed, but I heard the gospel preached in a new light, which made more sense than what my six-year-old self had previously understood. It was more about Jesus wanting a relationship with us, so I accepted the invitation, and that's when my life began to change.

Not long after, I got baptised, and my spiritual encounters filled with light. There was still a strong battle for my soul, and I messed up very often, made poor choices and embraced darkness because I did not believe I was loved or had worth due to various rejections and painful experiences. I kept Jesus as the one variable that I refused to let go of, and through the darkness, I would cry out to Him, and He would remain faithful. Our relationship grew stronger, and by the time I was nineteen, I had made Jesus my priority. This is when the real adventure began as He revealed more and more of Himself to me.

How it changed my life:

Encountering Jesus meant that I encountered love. In Jesus, I found a father, a friend, a saviour and a protector. I began to understand what peace felt like. I sleep well at night now. I am no longer tormented. I know what true joy feels like, not the kind that is fleeting with a gaping void that appears as soon as it's gone. I am talking about the kind that stays and doesn't end in guilt and shame. The kind

that allows you to rejoice and dance when nothing is going right.

I have a purpose in life and a reason to live. I became a wife and mother; both are to God's glory. I am continually being set free from various chains that I did not think I could ever break free from. It's a journey, and I have experienced incredible highs and lows with the Lord by my side, but I wouldn't change anything. He brought me out of every valley and danced with me at every mountain peak. He is indeed the way, the truth, and life itself.

III

Sandra Julian

My upbringing:

I was born in East London in May 1962. My parents were from Barbados. My mum was a nurse, and my dad was an underground train driver. They divorced when I was young. My mum and dad had four children: three girls and a boy. When my mum divorced my dad, she moved to Brent, and we lived with my grandmother (on my father's side) for a few years before moving to Wembley. When I was around six, my sisters, aged three and four, moved to Barbados to be looked after by our other grandmother. They lived there for seven years whilst my brother and I stayed with our mother. Mum decided to let me stay with her as I was a quiet, emotional child who had already dealt with much trauma. I used to cry every time I went out because of my parent's divorce.

I was very close with my father, but I always used to see when he abused my

mum. In those days, people never comforted a child when crying. Some members of the family would laugh at me when I cried. Even so, I was always interested in Church and used to go alone. Being in Church is where I felt peace. I never knew that was where God was leading me. I went to Church, a lot as a child with my mum. Even when I was older and more interested in going out to nightclubs, dancing and meeting boys, God was always in the background as I met with the Church of Latter-Day Saints and attended many of their events. I was eventually baptised there but soon discovered this was not my place. Then, I met a man who was to be the father of my children.

<u>When I met Jesus:</u>

I met Jesus when I broke up with my children's father after living together for around ten years. He met another woman and married her, which devastated me so badly that I used to cry myself to sleep every night. After putting the children to bed, I remembered reading a book called Letters to God, so I started writing letters about how I felt: heartbroken and melancholy. I felt so lost then, and I read Psalm 46 every night. Then, one night, I saw Jesus on the cross in my room, and he looked directly into my eyes. I felt like he shared my pain, and after that experience, I decided to serve Jesus, and nothing would stop me. My friend started attending the Methodist church soon after, so I also decided to join.

How it changed my life:

After that experience, I started to take the children and myself to church. This started my journey as a Christian. When I used to pray in my home, I always felt like dancing and had visions of ministering in the churches. The Lord would show me what to do even when feeling down. For example, I felt low, and the Lord revealed that I needed to dance. He gave me a song, and when I danced, the depression left. I felt God call me to dance ministry, which was also healing.

I was also suffering from Sarcoidosis, which makes you feel very weak and tired. I planned to go to work for one week and slept for two days at home, which meant I couldn't work a full week. But after six months, I was healed, and the Lord gave me a lot more energy to lead youth ministry and mentor many young people. Then, a minister gave me a word at a leaders' retreat where she said the dance ministry would start once I danced in front of the church. In 2014, we started the dance ministry named Vessel of Honour.

IV
Charity M Jumbo

My upbringing:

I was born in Nigeria but spent my formative years in Ghana, West Africa, where I received most of my education. When I was growing up, children's voices were often not heard. We followed instructions and were expected to adhere to instructions without deviation. Any deviation resulted in corporal punishment. This form of discipline was widespread, even in schools.

We were raised as Christians, but we barely made it to church. My sibling and I relocated to Ghana with my dad after living with my mum in Nigeria. At thirteen, I ended up living with an aunt and her family.

Despite my familial connection, I retained a sense of difference. I learned and figured things out by myself. When my mum joined us in Ghana at age twenty-two, I could not live with her as the bond had slacked. I had grown to be an adult in my own right and had become someone different from the person I was when we lived together. I was angry that she left me in the care of a relative I barely knew. My dad remarried and relocated to the United States. I finally had to live independently, and my younger sister eventually came to live with me.

I learned to fight and defend myself. I made mistakes and learned from them. I also learned from others. I thought I had no one to defend me if I got into trouble, so I tread lightly. I was excessively quiet and timid. I lacked confidence, and I was lost in myself.

<u>When I met Jesus:</u>

The first time I heard about Jesus was through our house help. The lady came to live with us when my Mum was promoted in her job and was required to travel, resulting in her being absent from home.

She was a prayerful person who constantly read her bible when less busy and lived righteously. Her journey with God could not go unnoticed even at my immature age; comparing her to the previous house helps.

We studied the word of God together, and on one occasion, I followed her to church. I went to the youth service, where I had the opportunity to give my life to Christ. My desire to know God better has never diminished since that moment.

How it changed my life:

My life is constantly transforming as God grants the grace. Over time, I have changed from timid to bold, from lost identity to knowing who I am in Christ. I have transformed from self-dependency to dependency on God. I am more reliant on God's word, seeing myself from the lens of God through His word. I am more forgiving, patient, and compassionate. I understand that God does not leave us unequipped after saving us. He fills us up with Himself, which allows us to walk and radiate like Him.

As we choose to walk daily with Him, He unveils Himself. Whenever you feel your strength has depleted in any area of your life, run back to where he met you in worship or prayer; you will be rejuvenated there. Do not ever take His presence for granted or neglect it. That is where our purposes are born. If you want to know who you are or your purpose, consistently spend time in His presence. No matter how short a time, just let it be consistent. You will understand who you are and what has been purposed for you.

For in Him we live and move and exist [that is, in Him, we actually have our being], as even some of your own poets have said, 'For we also are His children.'

Acts 17:28AMP

V

Siobhan Coker

My upbringing:

I grew up in a loving home in East London with my parents and siblings. We lived on the same road as a Pastor and often played out with their children. Naturally, they would invite us to their church. So, occasionally, my parents would drop us off at their church. As a parent now, I think back to that part of my life, and I wonder, "For my Mum and dad, was church just a free child-minding provision?" They dropped us off, picked us up, and ensured we had money for offering, but never stayed for the full service.

Either way, going to church was always optional. We were encouraged to respect everyone and their beliefs, but within our home, you said the Lord's Prayer before bedtime and grace before dinner.

Generally, my upbringing was straightforward in the sense that we weren't rich, and we weren't poor. I spent

a lot of time with family, had fun with friends and was encouraged to pursue my passion, singing.

<u>When I met Jesus:</u>

As you can imagine, when church is optional, it doesn't often remain at the top of the list of things to do in the life of a fifteen-year-old. However, one day, I received a message inviting me to a youth meeting, a reunion of all the old church kids who had lost touch over the past five-eight years.

I decided to go, and it was fun. I was then asked if I would attend the Sunday service, and I said yes. Upon entering the service, I was captivated by the presence of God. I wept and felt so moved by the singing under the anointing that I knew I needed more. After that, I kept going to the church, and they had a youth convention in West Bromwich, so a group of us decided to attend. Most, if not all, were coming for the

wrong reasons (a weekend away from parents)! But one of the services was so powerful that weekend that I finally listened to the sermon. By the end of the service, the whole church auditorium was filled with the presence of God, and before I knew it, the youth leader was holding my hand and talking to me about salvation.

My mind and heart were in a real battle. I gave every excuse as to why I shouldn't give my life to Christ. I remember saying, "But what if I'm only feeling this now because of all of this? But what about when I'm home alone? Will I hear God then?" She responded, "God is always with you, and when you accept Him, you ask Him to come and live in your heart."

Shortly after, I said the sinner's prayer and gave my heart to the Lord. It was a tearful experience with much emotion. The next day, we were in the final service of the conference, and the Lord spoke to me audibly. He said, "Go to the stage and tell the Worship Leader that he needs to sing Bow Down and Worship Him." At first, I looked over my shoulder to see if anyone else was experiencing this. I said to myself that I was not going up to the front but soon felt the Holy Spirit lift me by the back of my collar and poke me in my back to get a move on and walk to the front.

The worship leader leaned in close to hear me tell him that God said he needed to sing 'Bow Down and worship Him'. Immediately, the worship leader listened and sang the song. The church erupted, and people were falling out in the spirit, speaking in tongues, and it was an overwhelming encounter with God. At this point, I knew God was saying, "I am always with you".

<u>How it changed my life:</u>

This experience showed me that I couldn't question God, His Plans, His voice or if I heard Him. It was the evidence I needed that God hears, loves, and is always with me. It convinced me that God will use me if I am obedient.

VI

Laura-Louise Selby

<u>My upbringing:</u>

I was born and raised in an Irish Roman Catholic family that stretched back generations in Belfast, Northern Ireland. Everyone was baptised, confirmed, married and buried in the same church, and our community was very tightly knit out of necessity and survival. Growing up during a time of civil war meant identity politics, and British military occupation made the Christian religion the enemy amongst what should have been brothers and sisters in Christ. My city used "peace walls" to separate protestants from Catholics, and distrust and hatred bloomed from it amongst ordinary people.

My household consisted of a strong, loving father, an attentive mother, my little sister, and later two brothers a year apart. We were wealthy, wanting for nothing. My parents worked hard and gave us an amazing childhood despite the war. I had the privilege of being raised by strong parents who instilled in me to see people from their hearts rather than mistreat them based on prejudice. My mother went out of her way to teach us this, and it's no surprise that she later led the family to Christ through her open-mindedness.

<u>When I met Jesus:</u>

My parents moved from the city to a country home in a mixed-religious area without walls. When the time came for my brothers to go to school, my mother was adamant that they should attend a new, religious integrated system of schooling that was introduced after the military ceasefire of 1998. Through the school, she made a Christian friend, who slowly and softly introduced her to loving Jesus as a born-again Christian. She invited her to a small old-school prayer meeting run by the faith mission UK.

My mother continued to go back and encouraged us to come along. My father followed, and then eventually me. However, I do recall the stubbornness of the catholic identity keeping me from a salvation I desperately needed. If it weren't for my mother, I would have missed the chance to open the door when Jesus knocked. My mother and I were saved on the same night, and my father was saved around the same time but at a different service. It was an exciting time, having this newfound friend burn within our hearts, and we were eager to share the truth and love we found in him with our extended families.

How it changed my life:

It seemed our lives changed almost overnight. As we revealed to our extended family, we quickly realised they saw us as stepping into enemy territory, and we were accused of "forgetting where we come from". However, we believed we had found

who we were, and although the words hurt, we didn't claim them as our own. We went from having extended families of over fifty to just us six and Jesus. We were disowned and gossiped about in the local catholic churches and were visited by a priest and his girlfriend to ask my Dad why we left the church and why Jesus was so appealing. My Dad, being a biblical and straightforward man, left no words of truth unsaid.

We joined the nearest protestant church and struggled to find our place. We were welcomed but not included. They, too, saw us not as true siblings in Christ, and the old Irish saying "once a Catholic, always a Catholic" was branded on us. Eventually, after continuing to try to make it work, we had a home visit from the minister asking us to leave church as we didn't fit in. My Dad especially struggled with righteous anger after this because he believed fully in the love and truth of Christ's words.

However, we continued attending the weekly prayer meeting, hoping to find the right church.

It seemed like we were stuck in a cyclical pattern for fifteen long years of both spiritual and physical warfare, mainly because we weren't disciplined or supported as we should have been as young Christians. It was an intense time of loneliness, isolation, fear and sickness as my mother had lupus diagnosed in the middle of it all that rocked our family.

I remember being at work, getting on my knees and surrendering to God; if he allowed my family to grow and thrive, I'd say yes to everything he asked. This was the catalyst for God changing the season and the direction of our family.

I reached out to Hillsong, Ireland, to join the church and was met with a true representation of what God's church should be. I was mentored one-on-one by

the lead pastor in understanding a prophetic gift that God was unveiling in me. For the first time, I found real friends and felt wanted and loved by a community. God continued to finish a work in me to replace the trauma of rejection and renew his sense of identity, A painful but rich process. I met my now husband within two years of joining that church. An incredible man of faith, now living in London and expecting our first child, a son, in 6 months.

My brothers are much taller now, both saved, working on themselves and living Godly lives, which is almost unheard of among Gen Z, but I credit my parents' moral success. My saved sister helps care for my mother and is slowly rebuilding her life in God's way. My parents are thriving while Mum has healed and is healing still.

There are a million miracles I wish I could tell you; a million times, God has whispered into our hearts or broken ground in front of us. I don't regret how my story started because it built unshakeable faith. I've lost all things in Christ and have everything to gain. My aim is that one day, I'll stand before him and, having said yes to everything he has asked of me, leaving no stone unturned, will be able to raise my arms to hug my heavenly father and hear the words "Well done, good and faithful servant."

VII

Jackie Richardson

<u>My upbringing:</u>

I'm a daughter of the Windrush, born in 1960s East London to parents from the small Caribbean Island of Dominica. Our family was five siblings, often in matching handmade outfits, with grandparents nearby and a rotation of regularly visiting cousins. My upbringing was a mishmash of preserved West Indian traditions fused with working-class Eastend culture; my dad was a bus driver, my mum a seamstress for the local factories and Saturday morning pilgrimages down one colourful, noisy street market or another.

Back then, Christianity meant that I went to the local Catholic school and regularly attended mass throughout my younger years as I dutifully progressed through the sacraments like my First Holy Communion and Confirmation. So, for most of my life, I would've ticked 'Christian' as my religion when filling in any form, but

it was a distant adjective, and by the time my father passed away in my teens, church had become just an Easter and Christmas occasion.

<u>When I met Jesus:</u>

By my early 20s, I was a single mum but was still partying and dating when my younger sister "became a Christian". I didn't understand her new idea of a personal relationship with God when, as far as I was concerned, we were already Christians on paper. I teased her about how boring she was becoming as she seemed to be giving up on what was our idea of fun – staying out at parties all night – to spend more time at church and with her Christian friends. I always had an excuse as to why I couldn't go to church with her when she'd continually ask, until one day, I couldn't think of one and tagged along.

That visit wasn't the turning point for me that she probably hoped it would be – I decided I would never return to one of their "happy clappy" services. But my sister didn't give up, and I now know she was praying for me. I took my daughter to the church's Bank Holiday fun day in the countryside a few months later. I was relieved there was no bible in sight, just good company, field games and a barbecue. But towards the end, everyone gathered to sing songs about Jesus, and I began to cry unexpectedly. When my sister took me aside to find out what was wrong, I explained how I'd suddenly realised that something was missing from my life, and I wanted whatever it was that she and the others had. "That's Jesus in our lives", she explained before leading me through a prayer of repentance and salvation, giving my life to God.

How it changed my life:

Thirty-five years after making that decision - on the edge of that field with a group of cows as my witnesses - I look back and smile at how my life changed from the seemingly simple act of that prayer. Internally, as a single mum, I no longer felt alone; I knew God was with me, and He always would be.

My new peace didn't come from my circumstances, which were still often difficult juggling childcare with long workdays as a secretary and, at times, struggling to make ends meet. But knowing I could turn to God to give me strength, so many times, I saw his provision when I was at the end of myself, even seeing my mountain of debt wiped away.

Externally, I didn't know then that I'd also see God using me in a national women's ministry for ten years and then, for the last twenty years, in a healing ministry where I regularly see God answering prayers, healing, setting people free and touching lives. I'm grateful for my younger sister's perseverance and the church's creating a welcoming community event outside its walls, which would suddenly change my life.

We've seen more of my family come to have that personal relationship with God, which we first teased my sister about. So, my story is a reminder of the power of ordinary people simply sharing the Jesus they've encountered with the people in their lives, just like the earliest disciples did.

VIII

Teri Goodyear

<u>My upbringing:</u>

I was born near the East end of London in 1947 with an older brother. Like most families of that time, we weren't rich, but my father was an excellent provider. Although he was strict, I knew I had to keep to the boundaries set and not mess about! As a child, I could play in the street and our local park with my friends where we lived.

Our Saturday morning rituals of going to the cinema was a real treat! I watched noir movies, westerns, and new releases. Oh, the old days! I had a normal education and schooling experience; I went on to secondary school, leaving at age fifteen, and proceeded to start a hairdressing apprenticeship. Generally, I have fond memories of my childhood as a young, bustling Eastender.

<u>When I met Jesus:</u>

I had my first encounter with Jesus in Holloway prison in 1978. In 1975, after a lengthy courtship, I married the love of my life, John. Three years later, my nightmare began when I was charged with his murder.

I remember when we would hang out with friends at our local pub every weekend and drink until closing hours. Most times, everyone returned to ours, and the drinking continued.

One evening, we all returned to the pub; John and I had been chatting for yonks when I realised John had left me alone. This was so out of character! After looking around for him to no avail, I exited, got in the car and headed home. Only God knows how I drove home, as I was in a drunken state. We lived in a little village in Essex, and some winding, long country lanes are quite difficult and dangerous to drive on!

When I arrived home, I found John lying on the sofa. I was annoyed with foul words and emotions flashing through me. I went over and punched him. He sat up, saying, "You've stabbed me", and then he slumped back. I was confused, shocked and perplexed all at the same time. But looking at him, I could see and feel inside me that something wasn't right, and he needed urgent attention. I telephoned the police and blurted out, "I have stabbed my husband, and he needs help". Both the police and ambulance arrived together. John was taken to the hospital, and I was taken to the police station. I was signed in by a police officer and then taken to a cell.

I sat there numb and in disbelief at what I had done as I loved my John so much; he was my world, my life, and my all! That weekend would be one to go down in the history of my life as a never-ending story.

Sitting in the cell, I could hear footsteps coming and keys jingling. My cell opened, and the officer said, "Mrs Goodyear, we have some bad news for you. Your husband died this morning." I wailed, "No, no, no! That's not true." There was no response, and my cell slammed shut. I was shaking, completely petrified and traumatised with shock and fear. I could not move and went into a meltdown as though I had been plunged into icy, freezing water.

Everything was a blur, from the interview phase to the holding time. Twenty-four hours later, I was charged with murder and taken to Holloway prison to wait for a trial date. I wasn't coping, so I ended up being moved to a hospital wing and put on heavy medication for my safety, as suicide was the air I breathed.

My Christian friend Julie would often share her faith with me in the past. When she found out I was in prison, she came and visited me. I couldn't understand what she was saying, but one thing I did know was that I needed Jesus. Heading back to my cell, in my own way, I asked Jesus to help me!

Bless Julie. She never gave up on me and had her whole church praying for a miracle. With me being charged with murder, I needed one! Let me tell you, God showed up in my story big time.

First Miracle, I received bail for seven months. The condition set was for me to live with my wonderful and supportive parents. Through my state of grieving, I often had encounters with the Lord Jesus, who carried me through the difficult times ahead of me. My friend Julie put her life on hold for seven months, helping my parents. For the first time, I was introduced to the "truth serum" to help me unlock events from that day to get the

right support and aid my solicitors for the trial. After a horrendous trial experience, the second Miracle was that the jury found me not guilty of murder but manslaughter. Third Miracle, I only received a three-year sentence, which could have been much longer! The fourth Miracle was that I only had to serve one year in prison as I received parole.

Jesus became real to me throughout this ordeal at every hurdle, although I had moments of revisiting the past. Things didn't sit right with me and still used to haunt me. How did John get home from the pub on a three-mile journey down country lanes without a car? The police made enquiries, but no one came forward. The knife used in the stabbing was found by the police at the end of the garden, and my fingerprints were not on the murder weapon!

I have had to learn to put these questions to bed; the mental torture of how, who, and why will attempt to drive me insane, but I have resolved that Jesus, who knows everything, has forgiven me and loves me more than I can understand, and this has brought me peace.

Crying out to Jesus opened a healing process for me, where I had to be radically honest with myself, accept and love myself and embrace change. My Christian counsellor was fantastic and gifted; the shift began after two years of intensive therapy.

How it changed my life:

Through my healing journey, I shared my testimony with anyone I could, finding the Lord or, rather, Him beckoning me as I understood what the power of prayer and sharing has had on me. Surprisingly, I was invited to Premier Christian Radio in 1999 to give my testimony. After that day, I

received many more invitations to share my story with other women's ministries. My life has been one of service, devoting my time to serving at my church in Leadership mentoring and discipleship. Since opening The London Healing Rooms Ministry in 2003, I have been on the leadership team, facilitating and providing training to groups of individuals and churches who want to be the hands and feet of Jesus in our modern-day culture.

To anyone reading this, my one call to action for you is not to wait another minute with Jesus. All things are possible no matter what or where you come from.

You turned my wailing into dancing;

you removed my sackcloth and clothed me with joy,

that my heart may sing your praises and not be silent.

Lord my God, I will praise you forever.

Psalm 30:11-12NIV

Only Jesus can turn your story around,
for God never gives up on those earnestly
seeking Him.

IX

Sarah Andrea
Amissah

<u>My upbringing:</u>

I was born in Hackney and lived in Bow and Canning Town for my first few years. My mother, who had me at 23, showered me with love. Despite experiencing some traumatic events during my early years, I had a lovely upbringing. However, my innocence was stolen at the tender age of four or five, and this significantly impacted my perception of the world. Despite facing continuous advances from those who should have known better, I still managed to hold onto joy. I was a bubbly and playful child, surrounded by cousins and siblings whom I took pride in loving.

In school, I earned the nickname "the defender" as I always sought justice for others, even if it meant getting into a few fights. Some thought my approach was too much or misguided, but I understood that my aggression stemmed from pent-up anger and resentment within me. I was

also a creative soul, passionate about storytelling, a trait that became well-known among my peers.

When I met Jesus:

Growing up, my mother introduced me to God, who often mentioned Him and took me to church. However, I never imagined that God would know me personally or desire a relationship with me outside of my mother's connection. At fourteen, I began questioning and seeking more about God, spurred by conversations with friends and a desire for something more meaningful in my life.

My encounter with Jesus came when a friend returned from camp, sharing her newfound standards and transformation after giving her life to Christ. Intrigued and inspired, I desired that newfound peace she spoke of. During a pivotal moment after basketball practice, I was approached by a young lady named

Joanna, who asked about my afterlife destination. This encounter revealed that my mother's relationship with God might not be sufficient for my entry into heaven. Joanna prayed the 'sinners' prayer with me, marking the beginning of my journey with Christ, characterised by drawing closer to Him over the years.

How it changed my life:

Following my encounter with Christ, I noticed profound changes in my life. Convictions developed within me that I had never experienced before, and I found myself caring about things I had never considered. As I journeyed to understand God's love and embrace the healing available through Him, I discovered the grace to forgive and started recognising my gifts and passions, desiring to use them for the Lord.

Life wasn't perfect, but I learned that Jesus meant it when He said we would face troubles in this world, yet He had overcome it all. While it would take an entire book to detail the victories I've experienced with Jesus, I can confidently say that my life has never been the same since His love captured me. I am passionate about sharing the love and salvation found in Christ, aspiring to live more to myself and become more like Him. I have found purpose, knowing that I am known and loved, which surpasses everything. The assurance of my sins being forgiven and seen as righteous before the Holy God, thanks to the sacrifice of His Son, is a blessing beyond measure. Thank you, Lord!

X

Shan Lu

My upbringing:

I was born in China and grew up in a highly competitive environment. My parents had high expectations of me and made me work hard, filling my time with private tuition. I was obedient and made my parents proud by excelling academically and in extracurricular activities. Though I was the "perfect child" in the eyes of many, deep down, I was very insecure, and I wondered, if life is all about fulfilling my obligations and others' expectations, then is it worth living?

In 2004, I seized an opportunity to move to the UK to study, thinking I could start life afresh. However, I didn't realise that 'striving to perform' had become the only way of life I knew. Despite the absence of my parents' supervision, I was putting tremendous pressure on myself because subconsciously, I feared that if I didn't perform, I wouldn't be accepted as a person by others. This eventually led me to become an insomniac.

When I met Jesus:

I met the Lord in August 2008. A Ghanaian lady shared the gospel with me, and the Holy Spirit baptised me on the spot. I immediately started laughing and crying simultaneously, experiencing a sense of joy and peace that I'd never known before. I was cured of insomnia overnight. Soon, I began to devour the Bible. For many years I'd felt so alone, having no one to share my feelings with; I learnt to suck it up and soldier on when going through tough times. But now I know I had the Lord to talk to.

Little did I know that what had initially been an outlet for my emotions became a way to build intimacy with the Lord. I know I can be real and transparent with the Lord about anything, and He likes listening to me. Whenever He responds,

His words can calm the most turbulent storm, bringing peace with his perspective. This sustained me through all the seasons of my walk.

How it changed my life:

I have journeyed with the Lord through years of wilderness, where I had only Him to cling to, and where I learnt to love the Lord not because of what He promises concerning this life but because what He did two thousand years ago already proves He loves me. I have walked with the Lord through the valley of the shadow of death, where I experienced betrayal and abandonment from church leaders and had to learn forgiveness amidst excruciating pain. And the Lord was with me in the furnace, where all my childhood wounds resurfaced in the face of persecutions from my family, and where I overcame judgment towards my parents, learnt to love them just as they are, and became healed and made whole as a person.

Today, I speak, write, peach and minister as a passionate lover of Christ and a beloved daughter of my Father in Heaven. I've learnt that obedience is the secret to an intimate relationship with God. Suppose anyone wishes to grow in mature love and spiritual oneness with God. In that case, they must practise the words of Jesus which theology, revelation, gifting or anointing cannot substitute.

If you love me, keep my commands.

John 14:15NIV

"Whoever has my commands and keeps them is the one who loves me. The one who loves me will be loved by my Father, and I too will love them and show myself to them."

Then Judas (not Judas Iscariot) said, "But, Lord, why do you intend to show yourself to us and not to the world?"

Jesus replied, *"Anyone who loves me will obey my teaching. My Father will love them, and we will come to them and make our home with them.*

Anyone who does not love me will not obey my teaching. These words you hear are not my own; they belong to the Father who sent me."

John 14:21-24NIV

Obedience enables a person to experience the peace and joy of the Lord that the world cannot give.

Peace I leave with you; my peace I give you. I do not give to you as the world gives. Do not let your hearts be troubled and do not be afraid.

John 14:27NIV

If you keep my commands, you will remain in my love, just as I have kept my Father's commands and remain in his love.

I have told you this so that my joy may be in you and that your joy may be complete.

John 15:10-11 NIV

I long for every person on earth to know God's heart for them and encounter His raging love that burns for eternity.

XI

Jacqueline McGivern

My upbringing:

I was raised by my mum, along with three sisters, in an incredibly loving, stable and liberal household. As far as I knew, God was not a part of our upbringing. Through my teens and early twenties, it is fair to say I was the wild child and the youngest. This quickly escalated into alcohol and substance abuse. By my mid-twenties, I had adopted the "work hard, play hard" mentality, so occasional abuse turned into binges at the weekend. This lessened following my mother's diagnosis of terminal cancer, but my debaucherous lifestyle would continue shortly after she died.

When I met Jesus:

Following a brief illness at age thirty-two, I had the stark realisation that if heaven and hell were real, and I would have died, there was only one place I was headed, and it certainly wasn't heaven. I told God

that if He gave me my life back, I would give Him mine. I had no idea what I was doing at that moment. It would be a year later that I met Jesus. The Lord laid Himself before me that year, but I could not see Him through my stubbornness. I now know it is because it HAD to be Jesus - there was no other way. God saved me through the passage of John 14:6.

Jesus answered, "I am the way and the truth and the life. No one comes to the Father except through me."

John 14:6NIV

How it changed my life:

I traded corporate living for a life serving Christ. The Lord placed me in a Christian bookshop within the first three months of being saved, and I was placed amongst mature followers of Christ, which is exactly where someone like me needed to be (even if I didn't know it then). It's been

seven years this March, and I am free from past bondages - some were instantaneous, with the rest a journey of spiritual growth. I know it was all made possible through Him - not by might or power, but by His Spirit. Praise and thanks be to God!

XII

Kundayi Balogun

My upbringing:

As the oldest and only girl, I was to focus on my education and not bring shame to the family. Unfortunately, at the age of five, I was a victim of sexual abuse. I would sit flipping through an Illustrated Bible, talk to a man gathered by children (Jesus), and tell him about the bad man who did bad things to me. That bad man turned out to be HIV-positive and eventually died. God protected me.

Our home was traditional, and by my teens, I was still disciplined at times in front of or on behalf of my two younger brothers. They got to choose the belt I would be punished with. The last beating was when I fought back. I lost part of my front teeth. Academically, I was average compared to my brothers. I was depressed, suicidal and had low self-esteem. There was no point in being good, so I went out with the wrong crowd one night. My

naivety and mischief could have gone very badly, but God protected me.

<u>When I met Jesus:</u>

I felt troubled, not myself and vulnerable. I thought it safer to enter the cinema and watch a movie. As people settled down, the curtains opened, and a man appeared shouting, "Merry Christmas...!" Realising I was in a Christmas Service, I rose to leave, but a large hand pulled me back in my seat, and a deep booming voice that put the fear of God in me whispered, "sit down" .... "listen". I did look back. I saw two young ladies too far back to reach me.

After the service, I wanted to go home but was too scared. I asked God to help me, and immediately, I thought of getting my friend to accompany me home. He wasn't home, but his mum saw me loitering at her gate. After observing me, she said, "She's calling the Prophetess". So, I kneeled in front of two women praying in tongues. I knew because of a supernatural encounter I had experienced when I prayed in tongues.

Unfortunately, I believed it was evil, a curse or a punishment. Tongues were being stirred within, and I covered my mouth naturally. The Prophetess demanded I open my mouth. I remember shouting, "Pray!" and I prayed louder. The next thing I did was open my eyes and shout. "It's gone! There!" I saw a grey demon-like beast let out a piercing squeal and disappear out the window like smoke. I collapsed and sobbed in relief, joy, and shock. It felt like I had been locked up in a dungeon. I asked Jesus to save me, prayed with the women and was at peace, but I only discovered about five or six years later that Jesus saved me.

<u>How it changed my life:</u>

Unaware of my Born-Again Christian status, I continued as a Catholic. But when I moved to Europe, I overheard a bandmate say the sinner's prayer and casually mentioned that I prayed something similar before. That is when my journey with the Lord started.

XIII

Cara Olagundoye

<u>My upbringing:</u>

I grew up in Northwest London, an African Caribbean community in the inner city. I went to school, college and university, all in London. That was until I met Jesus.

<u>When I met Jesus:</u>

The journey began when I was eight, and my Mum became a Christian, which made a huge difference in our lives. We were a single-parent household and went from what felt like living purposelessly to having hope and joy. Even though I didn't understand what in and why, I just knew I loved attending church, having church friends and Sunday School.

My Dad left when I was six. There was an emptiness inside that I couldn't articulate. It was just a massive vacuum and space in my life and our home; he was the one who made a joke of everything, and with him gone, it was all so serious. Mum was understandably devastated and spent

days crying, whereas I never cried; I didn't understand what was happening because I thought Dad was coming back. I had this expectation for many years, but I don't know if my younger brother thought the same. He rejoined our lives after a custody battle to get visiting rights to see us, but we were never a family again. So, when Mum became a Christian, a born-again believer, it was a welcome relief; joy came to our home again, and it felt like life was moving forward.

Life did move forward for many years, then came my teen years, and we left what felt like the safety of our Methodist church to go to a Pentecostal church, where there were many young people, and Mum was to be the youth leader. I was unhappy about this as I didn't like the church! It was odd to me, and many people passed through, including missionaries, students and old members, but I found it hard to grasp what people were doing as believers.

It seemed people just came on Sunday and returned to the world on Monday, only to do the same thing again on Sunday. Even though I loved church and God as I knew Him at that point, I did the same: I listened to my secular music, went to parties and drank with my friends. But for some reason, I was mad at the church for being hypocrites! When evidently, I was becoming one myself.

Now I know the Lord was calling me, but at the time, I didn't, and amid the confusion, I was baptised the day after my seventeenth birthday. My family and school friends came. It was an epic experience as I kept crying, as did everyone else. We didn't know why, but even some of my school friends kept crying, and we weren't that close. It was a beautiful day, and I was changed.

The biggest change was the random chills I would get all the time, especially one time on the bus, which was particularly intense. Part of me knew it was the Holy Spirit, but I wasn't ready to acknowledge Him yet, so I prayed to God and said, "Lord, this has to stop; it's making me weird!" To my seventeen-year-old self, the worst thing you could be was weird! Nowadays, the weirder, the better, but at that time, I shut down the Holy Spirit in my life.

The nail in the coffin for me came soon after this when one of the pastors of the church took me aside one day and attempted to kiss me on the lips; he was over fifty and married with kids, so I was devastated. I could no longer go to church as the hypocrisy had gone too far. After that day, I left church, and the Lord, you couldn't get me to set foot in a church for many years. I thought that whoever would listen to church people were hypocrites and was vocal in my opinions.

These were what I would describe now as my lost years because even though I graduated from university and worked for some of the top companies in my field, I was angry and could only experience and give very little joy or love. Strange things would happen to me, and I knew that God was intervening and trying to remind me of who He was and who I was, but I wouldn't receive it. The whole concept of church had become a ridiculous joke to me.

My resurrected life came around six or seven years later. After I graduated from university, I got my dream job working in the head office of a top company, and I hated it! It was the most boring and frustrating thing I had ever done, and I thought, "Is this my life for the next forty years till I retire?" I often thought there had to be more to life than this. They were getting ready to make me permanent, and

I would be earning the money I'd always wanted, but it all came crashing down.

One day, I was getting ready, and I recalled that the last time I felt sincerely free and happy was when I was a child going to church. I decided in the mirror that I was going to church that coming Sunday to find out what this Christianity thing was all about. Just as I exited the bathroom, my mum was in the corridor and asked me if I wanted to go to church with her next Sunday. She had moved to a new church a few years prior, and I told her yes!

I went to church that Easter Sunday, and the Pastor preached the gospel of Jesus Christ. Every word he said felt completely directed at me and that he was speaking about my life. I was bawling my eyes out before he got to the end, and I remember wondering what I had to do to be saved. He gave the altar call, and before I knew it, I was standing at the altar crying at the feet of Jesus. It felt like it was just Him and me there.

There were around twenty or thirty other people next to me when I finally got up, many of whom were young. They gave us Bibles, and when I returned to the church hall, the Pastor's wife prayed for me. I received the gift of the Holy Spirit and spoke in tongues; they said I would need Him to get through the coming days, and I said that whatever it took, I needed Him. When I left the church, the world looked completely different. It seemed new and shiny, and it's been a new life ever since.

How it changed my life:

In every way, I am a wife to a wonderful Man of God. We have three children, are church leaders, run an international charity and run several businesses from the heart of England.

XIV

Dola O Opara

My upbringing:

I was born in France and attended primary school in Paris. I relocated to Nigeria with my parents and two siblings in 1996, and after finishing secondary school in Nigeria, I relocated to the UK.

When I met Jesus:

I encountered Christ during my secondary school years in Homaj. Before this, I knew God existed due to my mother's consistent prayers, yet I lacked a deep understanding of who He truly was. Our move to Nigeria initially granted me the luxuries teenage girls dream of—a spacious room with a lavish bathroom, starkly contrasting to the one I shared with my siblings in France. However, frequent power cuts and ongoing nightmares soon transformed my dream room into a nightmarish space. I grappled with constant fear to the point where I was unable to sleep or even use the toilet.

One day, a missionary spoke about Jesus at school, and I decided to give my life to Christ. I received my first Gideon Bible, complete with a table of contents featuring prayers for various situations. Previously haunted by dreams of oppression and snakes, I found solace in reading Psalms and following the recommended verses. Confidence blossomed in my dreams and in reality—I learned to call on Jesus wholeheartedly, and the nightmares ceased. It was then that I realised the reality of Jesus.

I began to pray, write letters, and converse with God regularly. Although I didn't fully comprehend God as a father at the time, I knew I had someone caring for me more than I cared for myself. My journey towards intimacy with God deepened after moving from Nigeria. People often say that teenagers face identity issues, and this was true for me, especially after giving my life to Christ. I grappled with feelings of

inadequacy and tried to please everyone, losing myself in the process.

After migrating to another country, I discovered that true happiness wasn't found in a change of location, so I engaged in activities and community work, yet the emptiness persisted. Cleaning church toilets and evangelising felt empty because my motives were selfish—I wanted to make it to heaven, but I lacked understanding about God's genuine love.

One day, overwhelmed and contemplating suicide, the Holy Spirit prompted me to go to church. The day was Pentecost, and I went with an open heart. The pastor urged the youth to seek the Holy Spirit, and at my breaking point, I cried out to God. I desired to see Him, feel His love, and truly experience His presence. That day, I received the Holy Spirit and an overwhelming sense of love, peace and hope. I had flashbacks of pain being

replaced with love, hugs, joy, peace and hope! It was an unexplainable feeling.

How it changed my life:

Since beginning my journey of intimacy with Christ, I have had hope and never felt alone. I have a righthand man always by my side.

XV
Pastor Christine Joda

My upbringing:

I grew up in a Christian home for which I am very grateful, and I am a daughter to two extraordinary servants of God and Giants in the Faith. They were pastors whom God used to significantly shape my life, the life of their generation and their nation. I don't have any horror stories per se, which I used to feel bad about, given that the most popular testimonies tend to be about extreme turnarounds. Mine was a turnaround in its own way, though. God's story for me was different. It's about a change from just knowing about Him to actually knowing Him, and that journey continues even today.

When I met Jesus:

I often used to wish my encounter with the Lord would have been more dramatic. As I mentioned earlier, I grew up in a Christian home, so God was a huge part of my life even before I actively chose Him. We were also in many powerful services, meetings, conferences, and around many mighty men of God from a young age, so to be honest, there were many encounters, but there was one I can relay.

One time, as a teenager, in my desire to know God more, I listened to a message on the protocol of God's presence and decided to implement the things I learned, and God met me there. I can always remember it. It marked me. I had gone into His presence thinking I would thank Him and then make my requests. I spent almost three hours just adoring God the Father and the Son; it was like I could see the throne room of Heaven. Afterwards, I was trying to remember what I had come in to ask for. Jesus was so glorious, captivating, and consuming that I was overwhelmed. This started the shift from just religious activity to a relationship with the Lord; I wanted to know Him for myself.

How it changed my life:

After that experience, I only wanted to serve God with every minute of my life. I longed, and still do, to see the name of Jesus exalted and glorified beyond just the four walls of the church but all over the earth. I longed for signs and wonders to be actively demonstrated, especially through my generation and in my nation.

I was aware of the presence of the Holy Spirit; my heart was to please Him, not to grieve Him, and even when I missed it, my love for Him surpassed my convenience and humbled me into making things right. Especially in situations when I felt I was right. Fellowshipping with Jesus governed my life and made it difficult to do things I could potentially "get away with" as if anything could even be hidden from Him. In a nutshell, Jesus changed my life, not so dramatically, but by my nature, day-to-

day awareness, and interactions, and I am
forever grateful.

XVI

XVI

Elizabeth Burke

<u>My upbringing:</u>

I was born in Dublin, Ireland, in 1948. My father and mother weren't married to each other. My mother already had a daughter, and she could not keep me, and her husband probably wouldn't have been jumping up and down about the idea either. My father's mother (my grandmother) was willing to adopt me. She was a very Godly woman of seventy years of age. What a brave lady. However, the Lord made this decision as she taught me about Samuel the Prophet and greatly influenced my life. Sadly, her children were affected in varying degrees by alcohol, so I saw many things NO child should see. The family pattern began to affect me, too; it was my way of dealing with rejection.

I began to drink quite heavily, not to enjoy drinking, but the effects to dull the pain had become a habit. I met my husband at eighteen, and planning to get married became a focus instead. However, when things went wrong, the bottle was always handy, and it became comfort and relief from emotional pain and rejection.

<u>When I met Jesus:</u>

Our eldest son Jon was born after Tom and I were married and around twenty-four or twenty-five. Tom was made redundant twice, so we decided to sell the house in Dublin and move to London. Jon was about fifteen months old, and Tom was already in London training for his new job. I had packed up everything for the move to London in two days. The phone was disconnected, and the television was sent back to the rental company, so there were no other sounds or people in the house except for me and fifteen-month-old Jon.

I was putting Jon down to sleep in his usual place at the bay window. I was about to leave the room when I heard a voice outside myself, about a foot away from my

right ear, speaking clearly and determinedly. "Move that cot away from the window." I was very taken aback. I moved the cot, and the next morning was shocking. Where the cot would have been, the floor was covered in broken glass, and a large stone lay on the floor, as somebody passing by threw it and smashed the window. This experience and the following vision changed everything.

One morning, I had a vision that was different from a dream. I was leaving this planet, moving upwards and coming towards what one could call heaven, and to my shock, I could not enter, and it felt like I was cast into a place of utter darkness. There are references in the scriptures about a place called outer darkness. When I returned to myself, I was shaking and soaked in sweat.

Now, I had to find out why I could not get in, as in church, we were told just to be good and it would be okay. Just be a loving person. I discovered that was wrong, so I understood that the Bible states clearly that unless one is born again, one cannot enter the Kingdom of Heaven.

Jesus replied, "Very truly I tell you, no one can see the kingdom of God unless they are born again.

John 3:3 NIV

One needs to accept Jesus, His death on the cross and the shedding of His Precious Blood. Him being the true Lamb of God and the eternal sacrifice for sin. He made the one-time atonement so we can be forgiven for all our sins and walk with him. Then, when our time comes, we can enter the heavenly places where Father God dwells.

How it changed my life:

As I got on my knees at home, I began confessing my known sins and then asked The Lord Jesus into my heart. I gave him my life and asked for His direction from now on and for His plan and purpose for my life to come into place.

The first thing I noticed was the peace of His forgiveness. I knew everything I had ever done that was wrong was forgiven, and my relationship with Jesus developed as He introduced me to My Heavenly Father. I now know that when I finally leave this planet again, I AM going straight in. My addiction to drinking and smoking was taken away that night, and I am now free of those addictions. I have seen The Lord change the lives of many as He did mine, and my relationship grew deeper and deeper. I have seen actual miracles, just like the bible says, and one day, we will be with the Father, Son and Holy Spirit forever.

XVII

Birgit Whelan

My upbringing:

In the beautiful poetry of King David, he describes God,

> *You perceive every moment of my heart and soul.*

> *You've cradled me throughout my days.*

> **Psalm 139:2; 22:10TPT**

As I remember my years as a child growing up in New Zealand, there is the sense of an enduring awareness of God, and of His loving presence. I do not remember a time when I did not believe in Him.

As a child, I was fascinated by spirituality and was especially drawn to Jesus. One memory which seems illustrative of this over those years is that at every Easter, the film 'Jesus of Nazareth' was played on television, and as a young child, I was compelled by this. I was captivated by Jesus and the story of His life, His words, His miracles, and His immense suffering

and death on the cross. And then, the joy of the empty tomb as He appeared, risen.

But over those young years, I also encountered other types of spirituality. At that time, I had no awareness or experience of spiritual discernment and my fascination with the spiritual world meant that when I was invited to clairvoyance and tarot readings and into other occult experiences, I was open.

And to another the power to work miracles. And to another the gift of prophecy. And to another the gift to discern what the Spirit is speaking.

1 Corinthians 12:10TPT

At eighteen, I left home and moved to another city to begin studying at Law School. Those early years at university were exciting, but I also faced some very painful experiences. One of these was the death of a friend. I was deeply distressed

by his loss, and I was invited to consult with a medium who, I was told, could contact my friend beyond the grave. Lacking in Scriptural understanding at that time, this possibility felt comforting in my grief. What I did not realise is that I would be drawn further into this spiritual world of the occult, looking for answers and for hope that would always elude me.

<u>When I met Jesus:</u>

I met Jesus in this darkness. Over this time of spiritual seeking in the occult, I experienced a kind of unravelling. I was looking for hope but felt more despair. I was looking for peace but felt more unrest. I was looking for answers but came away empty and desolate. There is a lot that could be said about the darkness that I experienced then, but in the end, I reached a point of being inconsolable.

It was an evening in the winter, and I was trying to finish an essay for university but

could barely see the page through the tears. I reached for the phone to call my mother for comfort. She said one thing that would change everything for me; "have you prayed?"

At the end of our phone call, I sat on my bed, with her question about prayer reverberating. It felt so strange. She had never said anything like that to me before. It had never occurred to me to pray.

I was unsure what to say but closed my eyes and spoke the Name of Jesus.

In that time of turning to Him in prayer, I received a vision.

In this vision, I was in a dark dungeon. I was on my knees, bound and desolate. I lifted my head and cried out to God. Immediately, there was a stream of radiant light that illuminated everything. I saw stairs leading up from where I was towards God. As I sat with this picture in my spirit, there was the sense of God speaking and saying to my heart that I was being taken from the kingdom of darkness and into the Kingdom of Light.

I would later come across these words reflected in the words of Scripture:

… and giving joyful thanks to the Father, who has qualified you to share in the inheritance of his holy people in the kingdom of light. For he has rescued us from the dominion of darkness and brought us into the kingdom of the Son he loves.

Colossians 1:12-23NIV

<u>How it changed my life:</u>

As I reflect on how my life has changed since encountering Jesus, I am reminded of the words of the apostle, John.

Jesus did many other things … If every one of them were written down, I suppose

that even the whole world would not have room for the books that would be written.

John 21:25NIV

These words resonate with my sense of a life of experiences with Him, and the many stories of His love, and His power, and His beauty.

At the heart of how my life has changed from that time is a love relationship with Jesus and a deep sense of being called to serve others in His love. I moved to the United Kingdom after university, and through a further visionary experience in prayer, I was led to serve in Christian television in London, where I could interview other 'ordinary, amazing [people], and how they met Jesus.' Through this time, I also furthered my understanding of theology with a Master's degree in Christian Spirituality.

As the years have unfolded, I have encountered many stories of suffering and pain in people's lives and have experienced some of my own. As these impacted my relationship with God, a deeper intimacy with Him and a deeper awareness of His tender compassion eventually emerged. I found deep comfort in the words of the Scripture:

The Lord is close to all whose hearts are crushed by pain.

Psalm 34:18TPT

What also emerged is the desire to reflect something of God's ministering love in the experience of our pain, as I returned to New Zealand and completed a Master's degree in Psychotherapy.

My story with Jesus continues to unfold and is resonant with the words of the psalmist:

He refreshes and restores my soul (life);

He leads me on the path of righteousness

for His name's sake …

Surely goodness and mercy and unfailing love shall follow me all the days of my life,

And I shall dwell forever [throughout all my days] in the house and in the presence of the Lord.

Psalm 23:3-6AMP

XVIII

Anne-Marie Rymill

My upbringing:

I am from the Midlands, England, UK, and am of Irish-Catholic heritage. Born into an academic and creative family, I had a strict religious upbringing and was educated in a convent school. I stopped going to church around the age of thirteen as I found it controlling and boring, but I was still searching for happiness. I found peace in nature and animals, particularly horses. I studied art, enjoyed music, and went to gigs, eventually joining the punk and heavy metal scene. I went on to study for my BA Honours in Fine Art.

Life became increasingly challenging, and I went down some very dark paths, but all the time, I was searching for the truth and the meaning of life. I investigated many religious, spiritual, and humanist paths. I had friends who were similarly searching, and I went with them to many new-age events, seminars, and festivals, but I hit rock bottom. I had never felt so lonely. I was in a toxic and controlling relationship, and I had no peace. I had enough of life.

When I met Jesus:

A friend told me, "I have found what we have been looking for. It's a course, and it's free, and it's at a church." I said, "I'm not walking into a church." But my friend persuaded me to come along. The church was Holy Trinity Brompton in London. I joined the Alpha course. I felt a sense of peace, later realising that it was the presence of the Holy Spirit, so I continued.

Simultaneously, I was trying to get out of a toxic relationship, but the person was very controlling and violent. Even though I had moved away, that person attacked me in the streets one morning on my way to work when two men instantly appeared out of nowhere. They were dressed in pinstripe suits and bowler hats with briefcases. One of them said, "Leave her alone." My assailant tried to argue with

them abusively. The other said, "He said to leave her alone." At which point my assailant dropped to his knees. I heard multiple police sirens, and they made an arrest. When the police asked me what had happened, I said, "These two men helped me." But when I looked around, they had disappeared. I truly believe they were angels and were sent to protect me.

<u>How it changed my life:</u>

I continued to engage with the Alpha course and was fascinated by it. On the Holy Spirit weekend, I had a powerful encounter when I surrendered my life to Jesus in a prayer. When people were praying for me, I had a vision of an empty cross with Scripture written on it.

I will never leave you nor forsake you.

Hebrews 13:5ESV

I had never read the bible, but later discovered that this was a verse taken from it.

I felt so much more peaceful and hopeful. The loneliness went, and shortly after, I also met the man who would become my husband. My life was filled with purpose when God said, "Will you paint for me?" This reinvigorated me to create and become a professional artist. I endeavour to present hope and beauty, unlock realms of wonder, shine a light in the darkness and worship my Lord and Saviour on a daily basis.

XIX

Oluwanipinmi Arokyo

My upbringing:

I am a Nigerian, born and raised in a Christian family. I grew up as an only child for years before having male siblings. My parents raised me and taught me the way of the Lord from home at an early age and during my formative years. My parents did a great job in exposing me early to Christ and the word of God as contained in the scriptures, making it easier for me to embrace the light of Jesus.

I was greatly encouraged to memorise and recite verses from the Bible, participate in the Children's Bible Club and read the Bible from a tender age. My parents were teachers and great disciplinarians, which moulded my life's moral and spiritual aspects. My parents equally valued Western education, making them invest in quality educational institutions to sharpen my dreams. They have always been very supportive parents and counsellors.

I attended a Christian Missionary Co. boarding school for six years during my secondary education, allowing me to meet and interact with a community of believers from diverse walks of life. It was a Mission School established by the Children Evangelism Ministry (CEM). I was raised as a disciplined child with the fear of God and the love of humanity. God bless my wonderful parents for a tremendous upbringing.

<u>When I met Jesus:</u>

As a child exposed to the gospel of Christ's truth, I have dedicated my life to Jesus several times. Still, I finally decided to stand for Christ after a sermon in fellowship during my secondary school education at Total Child School in Ilorin, Kwara State, Nigeria. I have been standing by my decision to follow Jesus Christ since then. Hallelujah!

How it changed my life:

My life took a tremendous turn as I began to hunger and thirst for more of a relationship and fellowship with the Lord, especially during my quiet time studying the Bible. I specifically received direction on my course of study choice from the book of Isaiah 42 during one of my quiet periods. By God's grace, I am a lawyer with a kingdom difference today against all odds. I became more conscious of living a life that pleases God and is free of sin.

I began to yearn for a deeper understanding of God's word through the scriptures, which has kept me in my Christian faith. My walk with Jesus has been progressive as I aspire daily to be like Christ, working out my salvation with fear and trembling. Praise God.

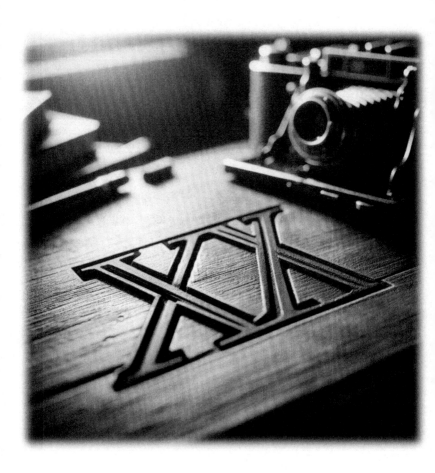

XX

Jemilea Wisdom-Baako

<u>My upbringing:</u>

I was raised in South London by Jamaican parents who knew God but were not churchgoers at the time. Yet, every Sunday, they sent my siblings and me to church with my grandparents every Sunday. I had a happy childhood and a good relationship with my little brother, with whom I shared a room. All the things I needed were provided, though we often struggled. I was a shy, introverted child who wrote her feelings down in books and wanted to become an author.

<u>When I met Jesus:</u>

Growing up in a Pentecostal church, Bibleway Church UK, I was immersed in church habits, practices and behaviours. As an observer, I naturally learnt what people expected of me - no trousers, makeup, or jewellery. To only listen to the gospel, read my bible and pray - I understood how to appear holy and wanted to be accepted, so I did what was expected of me. I knew scripture, hymns, and prayers; I loved God but didn't know him personally. My life had taught me that I had to earn His love by doing good things.

Once I left for university and had the opportunity to become anyone I wanted and partake in all the things that had been withheld from me, I was left with a choice - whether to tell people I was Christian. After a year of dipping my toe into sinful activities, I met Jesus on a Youth Retreat where, for the first time, I was encouraged to listen to God's voice and write down what He said. It was here that I experienced my first vision, where I realised that God's love for me wasn't just theoretical; it was tangible, real and accessible to me.

How it changed my life:

After this trip, I dedicated my life to the Lord personally. I spent time talking to

Him and building a relationship where I sought to know Him for myself. For so many years, I had relied on the faith of my grandparents to get me through, and being independent and away from the church I used as a crutch in my spiritual life, I became stronger in my faith and my walk with Him. This changed how I spent my time and how I interacted with others. It released my passion to serve him with my heart and be led by his voice. His voice has directed me through many life experiences, and although my life is not easy, it is a constant testimony of the glory and goodness of God.

Printed in Great Britain
by Amazon

37892456R00079